SCHOOLS LIBRARY SERVICE

Maltby Library Headquarters

High Street

Maltby

Rotherham S66 8LA

SEP 1990

MSC

(D)

ROTHERHAM PUBLIC LIBRARIES

**This book must be returned by the latest date entered above.
The loan may be extended [personally, by post or telephone]
for a further period if the book is not required by another reader.**

LMI

THE AMAZON

◁ MYTHS AND LEGENDS ▷

Translated by Abigail Frost
Illustrations by Jean Torton
Original version by Danièle Kuss
Edited by Gilles Ragache

CHERRYTREE BOOKS

A Cherrytree Book

Adapted by A S Publishing
from *L'Amazonie*, published by Hachette

First published 1989
by Cherrytree Press Ltd
a subsidiary of
The Chivers Company Ltd
Windsor Bridge Road
Bath, Avon BA2 3AX

ROTHERHAM
PUBLIC LIBRARIES

37239

J398.2

3345469

SCHOOLS STOCK

Copyright © Cherrytree Press Ltd 1989

British Library Cataloguing in Publication Data
Kuss, Danièle
    The Amazon. (Myths and legends. (Cherrytree
    Books).)
    1. Myths. Legends. South American myths. South
    American legends. South American myths and legends
    I. Title   II. Frost, Abigail   III. Torton, Jean   IV.
    L'Amazonie, *English*
    398.2'098

    ISBN 0 7451 5060 8

Printed in Hong Kong by Colorcraft Ltd

All rights reserved. No part of this publication may be
reproduced, stored in a retrieval system, or transmitted, in
any form or by any means without the prior permission in
writing of the publisher, nor be otherwise circulated in any
form of binding or cover other than that in which it is
published and without a similar condition including this
condition being imposed on the subsequent purchaser.

CONTENTS

THE COMING OF NIGHT

Long ago there was no night on earth. It slept at the bottom of a river, which was the kingdom of the Great Cobra. Only witch-doctors had seen it, in dreams, after they called up the souls of the dead. Night had no place in the world of the living.

At that time animals had not yet been created. But things – stones, leaves, tree trunks and even the warriors' arrows – talked, like people.

The Great Cobra's daughter left her home in the dark river to marry Takuña, eldest son of a village chief. Takuña had three faithful servants, who went everywhere with him. After his wedding, he asked them to leave him alone with his wife. When they had gone, Takuña called his wife to bed. 'I can't go to bed yet,' she said. 'Not until night comes.'

The astonished young man replied: 'Night? What's that? There's no such thing!'

'Yes, there is,' his wife said. 'My father holds it prisoner at the bottom of his river. Send your servants to find it – but don't tell them what they are to bring back. If they find out, they will fall under a spell for ever.'

Takuña called his servants and gave them their orders. 'Go to the Great Cobra's river. Tell him his daughter wants the big tucuma nut he has been guarding since the beginning of time.'

The servants trembled at the name of the Great Cobra. Nobody had ever dared enter the dark waters which he ruled. But obediently they went on their way. All the forest noises frightened them. They felt as if there was not enough air to breathe. At times they looked up at the highest trees, to catch a glimpse of the sky. The flickering light made the forest seem even thicker, and they were afraid of getting lost.

When they reached the Great Cobra's kingdom, he gave them the huge tucuma nut, and said in his alarming, hissing voice:

'Don't open it, or your live-ss are los-ss-t!'

'Here it i-ss! But whatever you do, don't open it, or your live-ss are los-ss-t!'

The three servants set off home, curious about their errand. What was inside the big nut? It had been cut open and sealed up with resin. They feared a spirit might be inside, maybe the one which suddenly appeared at a turn of the road to punish you. Or could it be a good spirit which helped the sick and hungry? They longed to open it, but the Great Cobra's words stayed in their minds.

They rowed their boat home without a word, fascinated by a strange noise. Inside the nut, something was singing: 'Ton-ton-ton-chi, Ton-

ton-ton-chi, Ton-ton-ton-chi . . .' They re-
membered the witch-doctor's chants.
'Ton-ton-ton-chi. . . Ton-ton-ton-chi . . .'

At last one said: 'I must know what's in
there! Let's open it! I'll make a tiny hole in the
resin, and slip in a straw – then I can look
inside. The Great Cobra and his daughter will
never know.'

'No!' cried the others in chorus. 'The Great
Cobra has forbidden it! He said that we would

die if we opened it!'

They thought they heard the menacing voice of the Cobra hissing somewhere. Thousands of eyes seemed to watch them through the overhanging branches. A strange light had followed them along the river ever since they left the Great Cobra's kingdom.

'Ton-ton-ton-chi, Ton-ton-ton-chi. . . ' sang the nut. 'Ton-ton-ton-chi. . . Ton-ton-ton-chi. . .'

What was inside the nut? The strange, piercing noise fascinated them more and more. At last their curiosity was stronger than their fear. Perhaps it was something valuable, which the Cobra thought they might steal. Or perhaps it was a good spirit which would work miracles, making them lords of the village. Even the witch-doctor would obey them if they brought new magic, stronger than his! Temptation and curiosity grew together. But still none of the three dared be the one to open the nut.

They stopped to rest for a while and lit a fire

Everything went dark, and the trees on the bank disappeared under a black cloud . . .

in the boat to grill the fish they had caught along the way. Still they could not take their eyes off the nut, which went on singing, 'Ton-ton-ton-chi, Ton-ton-ton-chi, Ton-ton-ton-chi. . .' Suddenly the youngest grabbed the nut and took it to the fire. The resin seal melted with an acrid smell. A splash of hot resin burnt their arms – then everything went dark. The trees on the bank disappeared under a black cloud which covered the land.

On the glowing embers, the only light remaining in this new, dark world, lay the tucuma nut, gaping and empty. The men could not speak. They looked at each other, as if to check that they were still alive. The oldest broke the silence: 'We're done for! The Great Cobra's daughter must already know we've disobeyed her father! She will put us under a spell. Our lives are lost.'

At the village, the Cobra's daughter was saying to her husband: 'Your servants have opened the magic nut, and let night escape. We

6

must sleep and wait for morning.'

She lay down at his side. As they slept, the things in the forest and the village changed. Stones and tree-roots became fish and water-birds; a newly-woven basket became a jaguar; a fisherman and his boat became ducks. Some things did not change, but ceased forever to speak. People could not understand the new noises that filled the forest.

But the Great Cobra's daughter was happy; now the forest was just like her home. When she woke up, she pointed out the shining morning star to her husband: 'See that bright light! It means dawn is about to break. Now I will separate night and day.'

She gathered leaves, flowers, grains, tree-bark and berries. She collected white clay in a jar. Back at home she knelt down and spread all these things out. She ground the forest plants in a mortar, and mixed them together to make different colours: a beautiful red, a deep black, and shades of blue, yellow and green. Proud of

her new paints, she wrapped a thread around her finger, saying: 'You will be the cujubin, the bird which announces day.'

She painted its head white with the clay, and its legs red. As it flew off she said: 'Go – and sing to us every morning as day breaks.'

Then she wrapped another thread around her finger and said: 'You will be the inhambu, the bird which announces night.' She took a little pot of ash, and sprinkled it on the bird she had created. 'Go,' she said. 'Sing in the evenings as night falls.' The bird flew off singing a soft, sad song. Then, looking at her pots of colour, she said: 'I will make my colours dance and sing in the forest. I will make all sorts of birds, as beautiful as the flowers and fruit.'

She began with a funny long-tailed bird, whose huge beak made the watching people laugh. She painted its feathers red and blue and called it a parrot. Tamely it perched on a nearby branch, trying to say its name: 'Arrrra, Arrrra. . .' The next bird she made had an even bigger beak. She painted it green, blue and yellow and called it a toucan.

The next little bird she made had a pretty red crest on its head. The next had fine blue feathers; blue was her favourite colour, reminding her of the sky, the moonlight, the rain and the clouds. For the next, she thought of the forest and all its greens. . .

Then it was the turn of black, orange and yellow; of ochre, beige and red. She made tiny humming-birds, red, green and blue. All her birds sat together on a branch, singing in chorus.

Suddenly they fell silent. Three men arrived, hiding their heads in shame. Takuña's servants had come to ask their master's forgiveness. 'You have disobeyed the Great Cobra!' said Takuña. 'You opened the tucuma nut and let out the night. You were warned what would happen. I sentence you to jump from tree to tree for the rest of time!' And the Great Cobra's daughter turned them into monkeys.

Even today some monkeys have yellow stripes on their shoulders – like the blisters from the hot resin which splashed the three who opened the nut.

All her birds sat together on a branch, singing in chorus.

THE LEGEND OF EL DORADO

On the high plateaux of the Andes Mountains, where the Amazon river starts its journey to the forest, there are sacred lakes, where sacrifices in honour of the sun-god were once held. One evening as the sun set, a sad sound disturbed the silence of the most secret lake of all. That morning, the village chief had made his yearly offerings to the sun-god. He had thrown the offerings into the water, and seen the shape of a giant serpent. Then he had returned to the village with his followers. He knew that that evening one of his wives and her youngest daughter would disappear for ever under the mysterious waters.

Next day, some Indians who lived near the lake went to see the chief. Everyone in the region was in awe of him. When he deigned to receive them, the Indians said timidly:

'Yesterday evening, we thought we saw the most beautiful of your wives and her little girl.

She walked sadly to the edge of the lake. Then we lost sight of her, but all night we heard crying. We looked everywhere, but could not find her. Her voice seemed to come from the water. All day a strange light has been shining under the lake, and the waters have been calmer than ever before.'

The chief knew he would never see his wife and child again. This last wife had been the most beautiful and noble of all. She had been his favourite since the first day they were married. It was almost unbearable to lose her in this way. The Indians' words made the chief desperate. He must get his wife back. The witch-doctor often performed miracles.

Perhaps he could help? The chief ordered him to come with him to the lake.

The witch-doctor sat down by the water and slowly drank a magic potion which would enable him to see the drowned woman at the bottom. He asked two Indians to light a big fire. Into it he threw some pebbles he had specially chosen. Then he paused, and uttered magic words. Suddenly, he stood up, put the hot pebbles in a little jar and walked into the lake. He threw the pebbles one by one into the water. They hit the surface with a hiss of steam and sank. Following them, the witch-doctor dived under the water.

The chief waited patiently for the man's

The witch-doctor said the chief's wife and daughter were happy in the lake dragon's kingdom, and did not want to return to dry land.

return. What had he seen at the bottom of the lake? He had seen the chief's wife and daughter; they were happy in the kingdom of the lake dragon, and did not want to return to dry land.

The chief was heart-broken. He loved his wife and daughter too much to be satisfied with this. He told the witch-doctor to go back to the dragon's kingdom.

This time, the witch-doctor returned from the lake in a state of terror. He said that the dragon was angry. He would not give up the chief's wife. If the chief did not give her up, the whole village would be punished. The frightened Indians fell to their knees by the lake, begging the drowned woman to protect them.

After that day, whenever anyone went near the lake, the giant serpent which lived there would transform itself and come out of the water. Each time it looked more like the chief's wife. Sometimes it wore a great red cape, and it announced all sorts of terrible things: deaths, illnesses, famines. Then it would disappear into a black whirlpool and the lake would become calm and silent again.

The Indians thought that only more sacrifices and more precious offerings would make the chief's wife intercede with the dragon and take their troubles away. They decided to talk to the chief. He had never seen the dragon's appearances, because he had refused to go near the accursed lake since his wife's death.

His people finally persuaded him. He prepared a ceremony which the dragon could not ignore. He sent his servants into the forest to find a special gum which dripped from a tree when it was cut. Then he said to his two best warriors:

'Go to all the villages which owe me obedience and take all the gold and emeralds you find there.'

Then he asked one of his wives to take her biggest pestle and grind a great quantity of gold dust. He ordered his best hunter to catch red

The golden man threw gold dishes in all directions. They shone like a thousand fires . . .

birds to make a diadem like the rays of the sun from their feathers. He had two very long ropes woven, and made a raft from wood that the witch-doctor chose. After giving all these orders, he went into his house. He stretched out on his hammock and calmly smoked a long pipe until the work was done.

Some days later, everything was ready for the ceremony. The chief, his warriors, his wives, his servants and the witch-doctor led the villagers to the lake. The chief asked four servants to take the ends of the two long ropes. One went to the north of the lake, another to the south, the third to the east and the fourth to the west. They tied the ropes to trees, holding them so that they rested on the surface of the water. The ropes crossed at the exact centre of the lake. Everything was ready; now they had to wait for dawn.

As the darkness receded, the chief got ready. He covered his body with gum and sprinkled himself from head to toe with gold dust. Then he placed the red feather headdress on his head, and put garlands round his knees. He put on huge earrings in the shape of discs, and a gold breastplate. The watching Indians jumped back in shock. He looked like the sun-god!

He climbed on his raft, surrounded by gold and emerald objects collected from the villages. He sailed across the lake to the centre point marked by the ropes. The Indians untied the ropes and drew them back to the bank.

Suddenly the sun appeared between two mountains, lighting up the whole scene like a firework display. The golden man – El Dorado, in Spanish – seemed to spring from the centre of the lake, throwing gold dishes in all directions. They shone like a thousand fires. The Indians thought it was magic.

The ceremony became famous. Tribes from near and far began to worship the chief's wife. The unhappy chief made regular offerings to her, and his descendants continued the tradition. For centuries, on certain mornings, just as the sun appeared behind the sacred mountain, a golden man spoke to the sun. . . .

THE SUN AND THE MOON

The sun's arrows were tipped with poison. His blowpipe was ready to fire. The god watched the trees intently for the slightest rustling in the leaves. Suddenly a burst of laughter made him look round. He had not noticed a young boy, who sat at the foot of a tree with two magnificent parrots.

The sun decided to relax for a moment in the boy's company. His hunting forgotten, he stayed there all day without noticing the passing of time. When the time came to go home, he could not bear to leave the two parrots whose chatter had amused him so. He offered the boy his crown of feathers.

The boy was just ten years old, and like all boys of that age he was very proud of his appearance. For the first time he was allowed to paint his body with black and red dye. His hair had been cut short, and when it grew back, he would have the right to plait and dress it. All this meant he was now a young man. He was already allowed to decorate his cheekbones! Imagining himself returning to the village with a beautiful crown on his head, he accepted the sun's offer joyfully and danced off in the direction of the village.

The sun hurried to show the parrots to his friend the moon. Enraptured by their beautiful feathers and delighted by their funny talk, the moon decided to adopt one. He chose the green one with a yellow head. He took it home and planted a piece of wood in the ground for it to perch on. The sun did the same for his parrot and gave it all sorts of seeds to eat.

Next morning the sun and the moon left together to go fishing with their bows and arrows. They also took harpoons, in case they saw their favourite fish, the pirarucù, which was too big to catch with an arrow. When they returned to their hut that evening, they were almost too tired to cook the fish they had caught. They stretched out on their straw mats and fell asleep at once. The parrots seemed sad to see them like that, and were silent all night.

In the days that followed, the sun and the moon could not understand why the parrots seemed sad. They did not seem to enjoy their talking lessons any more. One day, returning from the hunt, the sun and moon had two surprises: first the parrots met them talking better than ever before. They jumped from one shoulder to another as if they wanted to sing and dance. The second, bigger surprise awaited in the hut; two great bowls of steaming fish soup waited by the fire. Who had prepared them? They sat down, drank the delicious soup and went to bed. But they could not sleep trying to unravel the mystery. And the parrots looked at them as if they could say exactly what had happened, if only they could talk properly. Next day the sun and moon went out to hunt, their heads full of questions. While they were away a strange scene took place.

Gradually the two parrots changed into beautiful young women with long black hair which shone like a rainy night. When the change was complete, one of them hid behind the door to watch the two friends return, while the other cooked a meal.

'Quick, we haven't much time,' said one. 'Those two said they'd be home early today. We must be finished before they get in. They are so tired when they come back from hunting!'

Imagine how surprised the sun and the moon were when they came back this time! Astounded by the young women's beauty, they fell in love at once and begged them never to become parrots again. Soon they got married and held a great feast. But the hut was too small for four people, so they decided to take turns sleeping in it. The sun and his wife chose to go out during the day and the moon took the night. And that is why we never see the sun and the moon together in the sky.

The sun hurried to show the parrots to his friend the moon.

14

ANIMALS OF THE AMAZON FOREST

Anaconda

Tamandua

Vampire Bat

Giant Anteater

Puma

Red Ibis

Harpy Eag

Pirarucù

Cayman

Female

Quetzal

Male

Sloth

Armadillo

Leaf-cutter Ants

Bird-eating Spider

Piranha

THE KINGDOM OF THE URUBUS

Tamapù went hunting one morning, determined to bring home an urubu – a black vulture. He went to the lagoon, where the great birds loved to catch fish. He hid behind a tree and waited patiently. Soon an urubu came and began fishing. It was too absorbed to hear Tamapù draw his bow. The bird died instantly. Tamapù was proud; it was not easy to take an urubu unawares!

About to take his trophy home, Tamapù thought he heard weeping and went to look. There, under a huge palm tree by the water, was a beautiful young she-urubu. He decided to capture her and keep her. She followed him, tied by a leash and still crying.

From time to time Tamapù looked back at her. The bird had the face and body of a woman, and beautiful feathers. Why should he not marry her? She was much more beautiful than the village girls. As they approached his hut, he asked the urubu-woman to wait for him by the road, explaining: 'I must talk to my mother first, or else she will not accept you. What's your name?'

'My name must stay a secret, because I am the daughter of the King of the Urubus,' she answered. 'I shall wait for you.'

Tamapù went and told his mother he had found an Urubu princess by the lagoon, and brought her home to marry him. 'Bring her in, son,' she said. 'I shall accept her.'

Meanwhile the Urubu princess had plucked out all her feathers, and hidden them in a hollow tree. Tamapù thought her even more beautiful, and joyfully took her home.

They were very much in love, but they were not happy. Though Tamapù's mother agreed to their marriage, she was jealous of her daughter-in-law, and took every chance to reproach her. Life became impossible for the newly-weds.

One morning, as they went to dig their garden, Tamapù said to his wife: 'We must move away from the village. My mother will never get used to me having a wife. She will always hate you, and I love you too much to see you suffering.'

His wife replied, 'Follow me. I will put my wings on again, and we will fly up in the sky to

'Follow me. We will fly up in the sky to the kingdom of the Urubus. There we shall be happy.'

the kingdom of the Urubus. There we shall be happy.'

She took her wings from the hollow tree, and stuck them on with resin. Then, with her husband holding on to her shoulders, she rose up in the air. They flew up and up, over the great forest. Then Tamapù's wife told him to close his eyes as they entered her father's kingdom.

She stepped on to a huge staircase which led to a magnificent palace, so tall that the roof could not be seen. Suddenly Tamapù heard a grave voice and a clap of thunder.

'My daughter! You have done well to bring your husband here. Come to my throne, I wish to meet him.'

The Urubu king looked his son-in-law up and down. He sighed sarcastically as if planning something unpleasant. Then, in a lordly manner, he said:

'There is an insect under my toenail. Come here and remove it, but take great care. It has come to lay its eggs, and if you squash it they will cover my skin and make me ill.'

Tamapù took great care, but just as he got hold of the insect, the king moved his foot and Tamapù squashed its body.

'I warned you! You will be punished!' cried

the king. A half-smile passed over his face.

Tamapù was beaten and left lying in the forest. Three days and nights he lay there, without even the strength to groan. Then a rat came to speak to him.

'I saw it all,' said the rat. 'I live under the floor of the palace kitchen, where the king keeps all sorts of miraculous healing creams. I'll fetch some to make you better. Do not despair, I won't be long.'

The rat returned at night, with the creams for Tamapù's wounds and food and drink.

Next day the king sent his daughter to the forest to see if Tamapù was dead. She returned and said she had seen him in good health, talking to a rat. There was a clap of thunder, and the king's hand let out a streak of lightning.

'Go back to the forest and tell your husband he may stay in my kingdom and live with you if he passes another test. He must climb up the tree at the entrance to my kingdom and fetch me its biggest fruits.'

Tamapù did what the king had asked. The tree was almost too high to climb, but will-power overcame fatigue and he succeeded. As he came down with his hands full of fruit, the tree shook with laughter. The inevitable happened: Tamapù lost his hold and fell from the tree, losing consciousness when he hit the ground. His wife was there, but he did not see her. She knelt down beside him and covered him with leaves. Then she went back to the palace.

'Leave him three days and nights under the leaves, and then go and see how he is,' ordered her father.

When the day came to take the leaves away, the princess did not believe her eyes. Tamapù was not there. She ran into the forest calling for him, but there was no answer. Sadly she turned back. As she passed a little house which seemed deserted, she heard Tamapù's voice; he was talking to a beautiful parrot. She ran to tell her father the good news but he did not share her joy.

'Not too soon, my daughter! He has not yet passed all the tests I want to set him. Now he must make a throne adorned with my image.'

'But that's impossible!' she sighed. 'Strength and courage will not be of any use, because he has never seen your face. How can he put your portrait on a throne?'

'Those are my orders!' shouted the king, making the walls of the palace shake.

When the princess told her husband of this new test, his new friend the parrot spoke.

'I know who can help you. The woodpecker can carve wood beautifully, and will carve the king's image in a wing-beat. Say nothing to him; he must not know we are helping your husband.'

Three days later the princess returned to fetch the finished throne. It was made from a fine acajou-tree, and astonishingly like the cruel king. The king wondered if Tamapù had magic powers. The next test must be harder.

'He must build a house on the rock by the river, in the centre of my kingdom, using the trees which grow around my palace.'

Tamapù spent a long time felling the biggest trees and seasoning the wood. The rock was not

A huge eel rose out of the water and said: 'Don't worry, I'll help.'

perfectly flat, so he had to smooth it before he could start building. Then he had to make holes in it and fill them with cement made of soil, splinters of wood and resin, to hold the roof-poles. Tamapù made a special tool for this job; but the first time he tried to make a hole, the rock split in two, along its length.

He sat sadly by the river, not knowing what to do. Suddenly he heard a noise in the water. He leaned over and saw a huge eel, which rose out of the water and said:

'Don't worry, I'll help.' Then the fish disappeared. Tamapù saw the two halves of the stone rise up and stick themselves back together. He set to work again, but this time the stone survived his blows. He worked on cheerfully, not stopping to sleep or eat, afraid he might not finish on time. He called the weaver-birds he had seen at work that morning to help him. They flew about purposefully and soon had the roof thatched with woven stems. The house was ready – on time!

'There are two more tests for him to do,' said the king. 'He must make a clearing at a place I shall show him.'

Of course the king had chosen the place where the trees were most difficult to cut down, and the animals were most dangerous. Again, he gave Tamapù only three days and nights for the task.

During his tasks, Tamapù had got to know the forest animals. He knew they were often more generous and faithful than many humans. He looked around, and seeing a huge ant, asked: 'I know your people are hardworking and brave, and can do the most difficult things. Will you help me?'

'Of course,' said the ant. 'First, you deserve

The birds dropped their burning branches.
Tamapù was in the middle of a forest fire!

it; and secondly, we don't want that cruel tyrant to have the satisfaction of beating you.' The ant called its friends. An army of giant ants appeared, and ate away at the trees. They had little time, but Tamapù was happy. One more test and he could live with his wife!

When the ants were finished, the princess told him to wait in the clearing for orders.

Tamapù obeyed – but suddenly he realised what the test would be. Hundreds of urubus and other birds filled the sky above the clearing – each carrying a burning branch. Then they dropped them. Tamapù was in the middle of a forest fire. He spotted a dark hole, and dived into it, only to be terrified again. It was the home of a giant spider!

But the spider quickly soothed his fear. 'I won't hurt you,' she said. 'Listen to me! What a fool you are. Don't you realise your father-in-law wants to kill you? He will never let you live with the princess in his kingdom. Whatever tasks you perform, in the end he will kill you, believe me. But I can give you the chance to live.'

Realising he had no hope of a happy life with the one he loved, Tamapù sadly chose to save his life. The spider set to work, spinning silk out of her body, then weaving it into a cocoon big enough to carry Tamapù. He got inside, while she spun a long rope. Then she gently let him down to his own world below. He stepped out safe and sound.

But afterwards, whenever Tamapù saw a spider's web glittering in the sunlight, it seemed to him like a huge ladder. He wished he could climb up it, back to the kingdom of the urubus, to see his love, the king's daughter, up in the sky.

The spider spun a long rope, and gently let Tamapù down to his own world below.

THE ADVENTURE OF THE TREE-MAN

The wicked spirit Saruramà set the forest on fire. Just one man escaped alive. He survived by hiding in a hole in the ground and breathing through a hollow stick. Days later, when he dared leave, all was black and bare. There were no people, animals or plants to be seen. He was all alone; and there seemed to be nothing to eat.

Rather than starve to death, he set out westwards. He travelled towards the source of the great river where, according to the legends, his ancestors came from. He stopped in fright when a hideous creature appeared: Saruramà, the wicked spirit who had destroyed the forest. Did he now mean to kill even the last survivor?

Saruramà spoke. 'I'm sorry,' he said. 'It was wrong of me to destroy your world to amuse myself. I want to make up for the damage I have done. Take this handful of seeds, and sow them. You will bring back all the plants of the earth.'

Within seconds a forest miraculously sprang to life. From its depths the man heard a voice – a beautiful young woman calling him. He fell in love with her at once.

The couple married and had many sons, but only one daughter. The girl inherited her mother's beauty and wisdom. Her brothers protected her jealously, and she longed for a friend of her own.

One day, as she was walking alone in the forest, she met Ulé, who was half man, half tree. She fell madly in love with him. Every day she returned to see him. Her mother noticed she had changed, and that her walks in the forest sometimes lasted for days. She spent hours painting her face and decorating her hair with flowers and feathers.

The jaguar wanted to be master of the forest. Ulé fought bravely, but the jaguar carried him off.

In the end, the girl owned up to her mother, who said: 'If you really love Ulé, I shall not forbid you to see him, but be careful. Trap him so that he can't get away, and tell him he must marry you. Say you won't let him go unless he does.'

The girl took Ulé prisoner, but quickly released him when he willingly agreed to marry her. They lived happily together, until one day Ulé met a jaguar while out hunting. There was a terrible battle. The jaguar attacked the tree-man for no good reason – it was not afraid or hungry. All it wanted was to show off its strength and daring: to be master of the forest, feared by all the world. Ulé fought bravely, but the jaguar carried him off.

Ulé's young wife sat up all night waiting for her husband's return. In the morning, her brothers went out to search for him. She went with them, carrying her baby. Together they found her husband's remains – bones, leaves, branches and all. Kneeling down, she put them back together, and spoke magic words.

At once the sun grew very hot. A violent wind sent leaves and branches flying in all directions. Ulé's wife hugged him protectively, and closed his eyes. When she felt the wind drop, she looked round and, to her surprise, heard Ulé speak: 'I've been asleep for a long time . . .'

She had saved him! They walked homewards hand in hand, happier than the day they were married, because they had come so close to being parted for ever . . .

Thirsty after his adventure, Ulé asked his wife to wait while he went to a stream some distance away, through thick undergrowth. He bent down to take some water in his hands, but instead of drinking, stopped still and gazed at his reflection. Something was wrong.

At last he realised what it was; he had lost

25

part of his face! He dared not let his wife see him like that. Hiding his changed face in his hands, he ran back to her. Although she tried to tell him that she had already noticed, and it did not matter, he begged her to go home alone. He would stay behind and look for the missing part of his face. She must not look back, whatever she heard behind her. In the thick forest, it was easy to forget your direction and get lost for ever.

Ulé's wife travelled sadly on. The forest made many sounds, but she knew them all, and did not look back. But suddenly, just behind her, a leaf fell with an unusual sound. The young woman spun round, wondering what the strange noise could be. In that instant she lost her direction. She wandered for hours, until night fell. Then she lay down with her baby in her arms. Exhausted by thirst and sorrow, she quickly fell asleep.

When she woke, she had a shock. Stretched out beside her was the mother of the jaguars, whose lair she had slept in all night. The jaguar looked at her kindly.

'I let you sleep a while,' she said, 'but now I must hide you away. My sons will be home soon, and they are very cruel. I fear that they will kill you and your baby.'

When the young jaguars returned from hunting, they soon noticed the smell of humans in the lair. They made their mother tell them where she had hidden the people. Then they killed the young woman, took the baby and put him in a big clay pot:

'Let's stew it with insect-grubs and roots. It will make a wonderful soup,' they joked to their mother.

The mother of the jaguars pretended to agree, but while her sons slept she swapped the baby for a piece of meat. She hid him in a tree and went to sleep beside him.

Each day, while her sons were out, she fed the baby, licked him and played with him until night fell. She called him Tiri.

Tiri grew up and became a man. He began to hate his hiding-place, feeling as if he were a prisoner. He took to going into the forest trying to hunt. One day he caught a little mouse, but so clumsily that he only broke its tail off. He followed it for a while, knowing that the mother of the jaguars was cross with the little animal for stealing from her larder. At last he cornered the mouse, but it turned round and said:

'Why do you want to harm me? I've done nothing to you. But you are serving your mother's killers!'

Tiri did not understand. He could not remember the terrible things that had happened when he was a baby. The mother of the jaguars, ashamed, had never mentioned her sons' crime. The mouse told him the whole story.

Tiri went back to the jaguars' lair, to wait for them – and revenge. The first three did not realise he was after them, and he killed them with no difficulty. But the fourth had time to hide in a tree and call the moon and stars to his aid. The moon took pity and hid him from Tiri. (Some people think you can still see a jaguar hiding in the moon.) Tiri went to the mother of the jaguars and said: 'You are not guilty and have nothing to fear. You have been kind to me; now I will look after you.'

It turned out that Tiri had magic powers, and he became master of the forest. He cleared a plot of land to plant crops. But he was lonely, so he made a friend for himself, called Karou. Walking in the forest one day, the two friends found a snake-spirit sleeping at the entrance to a big hole in the ground. Tiri asked the falcon Uaccauan to kill the snake-spirit, and then unblocked the hole.

Out of it rushed a crowd of people, like a river overflowing in the rainy season. The people were of all shapes, sizes and colours – they were the different tribes of the world. They spread out to all the corners of the earth. Tiri knew they would soon be at war. He made arrows rain down from the sky, and gave some to all the tribes.

Now that the world was full of people, Tiri's task was over. He walked away towards the setting sun.

Each day, the jaguar-mother fed the baby, licked him and played with him until night fell.

THE COMING OF FIRE

The people who lived at the beginning of time did not know about fire. They ate their meat and fish raw, and had nothing to keep them warm on cold nights. Two fishermen who were sleeping one night on a rock in the middle of the river were woken by a heavy storm. Rain fell in sheets, and the shivering men looked up at the sky. It was hours before sunrise, but little by little they felt warm. They could not understand it. The night was as dark as the bottom of the great river. The rain had stopped, but surely only the sun could make them warm again. Why weren't they cold? But they were tired, and despite their curiosity, they slowly went back to sleep.

When they awoke the sun was well up. They could smell something strange which they did not recognize. Wondering what it could be, they climbed into their boat thinking they had been dreaming.

As they rowed along another surprise made them stop. All around fish were floating on the surface of the water! And the fish were not their usual colour – the fishers knew their shapes,

A warm wind rose up. Suddenly they saw a strange light moving towards them, over the water.

but otherwise they were different. What a strange night! They took some fish, and nibbled at them cautiously.

They were astonished by the taste. 'It's delicious! Better than anything we've had before! The flesh is so tender. We must stay here and watch to see what has happened.'

They went back to the rock and spent the day gathering shellfish. Their tribe used the rarest, most beautiful shells for jewellery, and for money too. Some other tribes used birds' feathers in the same way. As they feasted on the strange fish, they talked about the mysterious heat that came without sun. They had to learn its secret, if only because they no longer liked the taste of raw fish. And their lives would be so much better if night was no longer cold.

They sat up talking and watching each other to make sure that neither dropped off to sleep. In the middle of the night, just as before, a huge storm broke and left them shivering on the rock. Then gradually a warm wind rose up, taking away the chill. Suddenly they saw a strange light over the water. As it moved towards them, it seemed to take on a human shape. They could make out a face, then a body, and, as the light came over their rock, it became a young man. His body gave out a vivid warmth, as though one of the sun's rays had come to earth.

The fishermen were paralysed with fear. Was he one of the sun's children? Had he come to

They took turns to row and tend the fire.

and threw them on the fire to keep it burning.

At dawn the fire was still alive, and they had plenty of wood. Could they take it with them? 'Come on! One row and the other look after the fire! This is the Mother of Fire; it will feed us and warm us as if we were its children. It will be our tribe's new mother.'

Now they had to find a way to take it home in their wooden boat. Cleverly, they made a hearth with a hollow stone, and pushed the ball of fire in it with more stones. They placed shells around it, to stop it falling out if the boat rocked. Then they loaded their fire-wood, untied the mooring-rope and pushed off. They took turns to row and tend the fire. When they saw their village, night was falling.

Their friends and families were waiting on the river-bank, worried by their delay. Sitting in the darkness, they could not make out the boat at first. All they could see was a bright light which seemed to float down the river.

They ran back to the village in great excitement. 'A star has fallen from the sky and is coming towards us down the river!' they cried. 'No, that can't be it,' said others. 'It's the Mother of the Water. She must be angry with us.'

The men took their bows, arrows and blow-pipes to defend themselves. The women hid their children, then they too took up weapons. The whole village panicked, running in all directions.

Meanwhile, the two fishermen had landed. The villagers saw their shapes against the mysterious light. Then they recognised them. Still a little worried, but intrigued, they went up to the men, astonished at what they had brought. It seemed to be the sun.

The fishermen told their story. The villagers listened in the fire's pleasant warmth. Then the chief spoke: 'We must go home and sleep. Each family in turn will look after the Mother of Fire. Any who fail in this duty will be punished. And that's not all. The spirits of cold under the water will surely try to put the fire out. We must take care of it. Wood alone will not give it

punish them or to help them? Why was he standing there, silent, looking straight at them? What did he want?

Suddenly one fisherman grabbed at the stranger's hair. In a fraction of a second, the young man disappeared into the water. The brave fisherman stopped open-mouthed; at his feet shone a ball of fire – all that was left of the young stranger.

He tried to pick it up in his hands but it burnt him. His friend tried to lift it with sticks of wood, but the sticks burst into flames. This gave them an idea; they gathered dry branches

30

strength to survive the spirits' attacks. At every new moon we must return to the rock where it was found and wait for the Light, to try and capture it. We will all fight these bad spirits together.'

The villagers did not worry. They loved the wonderful warmth, and quickly discovered the delicious taste of cooked fish. Having heard about it from the fishermen, they could not wait to try it for themselves.

Until the night of the new moon, the villagers enjoyed life. They learned to cook meat and thought up a new recipe every day, boiling all sorts of roots, leaves, grubs and insects in water to make soup. One day they might add pepper, or turtle-oil . . . They completely forgot the chief's orders.

But a month later the chief led them to the water. It was time to go back to the rock, wait for the light and capture a flame to revive the fire. Two young warriors set sail with the chief, the witch-doctor, and the fishermen. The party never returned. But in the village, the fire never went out. It glowed day and night for ever after.

'A star has fallen from the sky! It's coming towards us!'

▷THE SNAKE ARROWS◁

Two huge monkeys were terrorising the island of Bananal, catching people and eating them up. Two brothers set out with bows and arrows to rid their village of the monsters. A frog by the side of the road asked where they were going. 'We're going to kill the man-eating monkeys,' they replied boldly. 'We're not afraid of them!'

'You haven't got a chance,' said the frog. 'I'm not going to help you.'

But the two brothers, as proud as they were brave, ignored the little frog and went on their way. A short way from the monkeys' tree they felt a chill down their spines: the ground was covered with human bones. The monkeys, grinning, watched them arrive, then jumped down on the fearless pair. They met the same end as so many others – eaten up.

Back at the village their younger brother Marikà lay on a straw mat. He stared at the path to the river which they had taken. The sun had set, and they should have returned by now. He was too ill to go and meet them. His body was covered with infected wounds, which the witch-doctor could not heal.

Next day, his brothers were still gone and there was nothing to eat. Marikà got up painfully and took his bow and arrows from their hook on the roof-pole. He thought he might be strong enough to catch a few birds, whose feathers he could exchange for food. With luck, he might kill a peccary. But he did not have the strength. The walk to the forest alone wore him out.

Then he saw a parrot, and stumbled, distracted, into a snake's hole. The snake came out crossly and said: 'What are you doing in the forest in your state of health? Go back to bed at once! You're a danger to yourself and others!'

'What else can I do?' replied Marikà. 'I'm all alone in the world now. My brothers went to kill the man-eating monkeys, and have not returned. They must have been eaten up. I have no one to look after me or bring me food. If I don't go out to hunt I will die.'

The snake took pity on him and said: 'I'll give you some ointment to heal your wounds, but you mustn't tell anyone I did it.'

The snake spread thick black paste from a clay pot over Marikà's body. When Marikà got home, everyone was astonished to see him walk without pain, and asked about the black stuff on his skin. He said it was covered in soot from some burnt trees.

Three days later he felt well enough to avenge his brothers, and set out to find the monkeys. His friend the snake gave him a strange present:

'This magic arrow will help you get revenge. On your way you will meet a frog. She will ask you to marry her. Pretend to accept, and she will tell you a secret, which will let you kill the monkeys.'

Marikà left on his quest, prepared to do whatever he had to in revenge. The magic arrow gave him confidence. Just as the snake said, the little frog stopped him. She asked him to marry her, and he said that he would. Then she told him about the monkeys' weak spot – their eyes. If he could pierce their eyes with an arrow, they would die. Marikà thanked the frog warmly and asked her to wait until he returned.

Marikà reached the tree. The scattered bones did not scare him, but made him more eager to

The monkeys laughed, but Marikà stood still and shot.

kill. Nothing could stop him now.

The monkeys laughed at his boldness, and came out on the attack. Marikà was not bothered. He gazed straight into the monsters' eyes, standing perfectly still. Swift as lightning, he shot his arrow into the bigger one's eye. As it fell dead, the magic arrow flew back to the bow – then out again, straight into the other monkey's eye. Both man-eaters lay dead under the tree.

The young warrior returned and told his story to the snake, who gave him a quiver full of arrows, explaining: 'There is a special one for each animal. These arrows are magic – they never miss their target and will return to your hand after the kill. But if they are used by anyone else, their power will be evil. If that happens, use this secret spell to take their power away.' Then the snake whispered what Marikà must do.

With his magic arrows, Marikà became the best hunter in the village, never coming home empty-handed. His friends grew jealous.

Marikà got married to a village girl. He built a house, cleared some land, and planted cassava, maize, peanuts and tobacco, and plants which gave colours to paint his face with. He warned his wife not to let anyone else touch his arrows.

But his wife's sly brother persuaded her to lend him the magic arrows. While Marikà worked on his land, his brother-in-law took the arrows and went hunting. He returned to hang them up on their hook before the owner got home. Marikà suspected nothing.

One day a spirit with a huge mouth and hundreds of teeth appeared in the forest. Marikà's brother-in-law fled in terror, leaving the arrow he had just shot. The spirit pursued him to the village, where it killed everyone it

could catch. People ran, hid and begged for mercy, all in vain; the greedy spirit spared no one. Marikà, hearing all the noise, ran home.

This was what the snake had warned him about. Sadly, he said the words that would take away his arrows' magic power. The spirit vanished with a noise like thunder.

Marikà was safe, though no longer powerful. But most of the villagers were dead; and those among the living who had glimpsed the creature's huge mouth and teeth could never forget the horrible sight.

While Marikà worked on his land, his brother-in-law took the arrows and went hunting.

DENAKE AND THE STAR

Long ago the Carajas did not know how to grow plants. They lived by hunting, fishing and gathering fruit. They could not dig a plot of ground to plant maize, cassava or pineapple. In the rainy season, they sometimes went for days with nothing to eat.

Two sisters lived in a Caraja village: Imahero, the elder and Denake, the younger. One evening they were looking at the stars with their father, who was telling them legends. Imahero had a strange sensation; she could not take her eyes from the biggest star in the sky.

'What's that shining up there?' she asked her father. 'I want it.'

Her father laughed.

'That's the great star Tahina-Can. It's much too far away for you to reach. But perhaps if it is your heart's desire you can have it: if it hears you calling and wants to come and live with you, your wish may come true.'

The girl fell asleep thinking only of Tahina-Can.

Late at night she was alarmed by the sound of someone coming in to the house, and called out: 'Who's there?'

'It's Tahina-Can!' came the reply.

Breathless with joy, Imahero saw a light shining in the darkness and ran towards it. She called her father and sister, and lit a fire to see what Tahina-Can looked like. To her disappointment she found that the star which lit up the sky was only an old man. His white beard and hair glowed in the light of the fire. Angrily she cried: 'Go away! I don't want to marry you. You're too old and ugly. Go away.'

Tahina-Can turned round and started to cry

Imahero could not take her eyes from the biggest star in the sky.

softly. Denake went to him, took his hands and said: 'I will marry you. I would like you to be my husband.'

The old man was very happy. The wedding took place next day. The morning after, the old man said to his pretty young wife:

'Now I will go into the forest and plough up some land, and plant good things for you, plants the Carajas have never seen. But I must go alone.'

He went down to the river, and said magic words to it. Then he walked into the water up to his knees, leaning into the current. From time to time he plunged his hand into the water and pulled out seeds of maize, cassava and all the other plants which the Carajas now grow. Then he went into the forest to clear his plot of land.

Denake was worried when he did not return. He was too old and weak to work very hard. Something must have happened to him, perhaps he was injured . . . Unable to bear it any longer, at nightfall she decided to disobey, and go to meet him. At last she saw a young man raking through hot ashes on the ground.

'Have you seen an old man?' she asked. 'He's my husband and I am very worried because he has not come home. I am afraid something has happened to him.'

'I am Tahina-Can,' replied the handsome young man. 'I am not really an old man, but made myself look like one to test your sister's love. I learnt the truth that way. I was delighted that you would marry me despite what I looked like, and to reward your generosity I have given your people all these plants. Let's go back to the village and tell them.'

When Tahina-Can had finished his story, Imahero screamed and fell down in a faint. A few seconds later, her body disappeared and a wild bird appeared in her place. Ever since, when the stars come out, the bird has wailed sadly.

The star which lit up the sky was only an old man.

THE CRAB AND THE JAGUAR'S EYES

For days the jaguar had been watching a crab. He could not believe what he was seeing. The crab was sending his eyes for a walk by the lake.

'Fly eyes, fly to the lake! Fly, fly, fly!' he said. And his eyes would pop out and fly towards the lake like butterflies.

After a while, he would call them back: 'Come back, eyes, come back at once!'

The jaguar could keep quiet no longer. He went to the crab and said:

'What are you doing?'

'Look: I'll show you. Fly eyes, fly to the lake!' And off flew his eyes to the edge of the lake.

'Come back, eyes, come back at once!'

And his eyes returned at once.

The jaguar wanted to do the same trick, and asked the crab to send his eyes to the lake. The crab refused:

'Not now, the monster will eat them.'

'I want you to send them.'

'All right,' said the crab, 'but be warned!'

And he sent the jaguar's eyes to the lake. After a moment, he called them back: 'Come back, jaguar's eyes, come back at once!' And they flew back into their sockets.

'That's wonderful, send them back again,' said the jaguar.

'No, it's not safe now,' replied the crab. 'The monster's coming, he'll eat them up.'

'Please, please, just one last time.'

The crab gave in. But he had been right when he said no. The monster was there, and it ate the jaguar's eyes. The crab spoke his magic words, but the eyes did not return. The jaguar was blind. Enraged, he threatened to eat the crab, who hid under the root of a tree. The jaguar scraped at the root, but could not find the crab. He could no longer see, and to his claws, the crab's shell felt just like wood. That is why some of the Amazon crabs have stripes on their shells, from the jaguar's claws.

The jaguar wandered through the forest, not knowing where he was going. Unable to hunt without eyes, he was doomed to starve to death. He stopped under a tree and lay down to sleep. What could he do? A sparrow-hawk halted nearby and asked: 'What's happened to you, where are your eyes?'

The jaguar told him his strange story, which the sparrow-hawk could hardly believe. He

decided to help the poor blind jaguar.

'Wait here,' he said. 'I will find what we need to get to make you new eyes. Hide your head between your paws, so that other animals cannot see you are blind; then you'll be safe. They're all afraid of you and won't dare approach. I will bring back some jatoba-sap, which hardens if you heat it up.'

Hours later the jaguar heard a great noise. The sparrow-hawk had dropped beside him everything he had brought to make his new eyes. He told the jaguar:

'Stretch yourself out and stay still. This will hurt, but you must bear it.'

He heated the jatoba-sap, then said: 'Don't move!' He poured the boiling liquid into the jaguar's right socket. The jaguar did not even flinch. Then he poured it into the left socket, and left it to harden into new eyes. Then he washed the eyes with the sap of a tree.

The jaguar's new eyes were very bright, and even more beautiful than his old ones.

'How can I repay you?' said the jaguar.

'Just kill me a tapir – my favourite meat.'

The jaguar went straight out to hunt. He caught a huge tapir, which his new friend enjoyed very much.

Ever since that day, the jaguar always leaves a part of his kill for the sparrow-hawk, in gratitude for his new eyes.

'The monster's coming, he'll eat your eyes up!'

THE MYSTERY OF THE SIERRA

Mahimbo chewed his plug of tobacco, staring straight ahead at the fire burning under a pot of alligator soup. He kept thinking about the strange and frightening thing which had happened last time he went hunting with his friends. He was so preoccupied that he hardly saw his wife and daughters come home with their harvest of fruit and berries, or heard their necklaces of seeds rattling on their chests like dozens of little bells.

Without a word, Mahimbo ate his soup and went out as usual to the forest. There he sat on an old tree-stump, looking up at the high mountain peaks of the Sierra. Soon he was lost in his thoughts again.

His tribe never went high up on the mountains. But on the day of the hunt he had got lost in the forest, and wandered upwards until he reached a lonely village. He did not know the people. Their hairstyle and the patterns on their faces were strange. Not sure he would be welcome, he hid behind a tree.

What he saw did not reassure him. After eating and drinking tea, the people danced and sang in the centre of the village, as if worshipping their gods. Suddenly an enormous black puma advanced towards them, crouched down and, yawning nonchalantly, began to look around as if waiting for someone or something.

The people danced round the black puma, stopped, saluted it with incantations and began their ritual dance again. Suddenly a horrible creature, neither human nor animal, arrived. Was it a monkey which walked and acted like a man, or a man with shaggy fur and animal's paws? It was this creature the puma was waiting for. The monkey-man approached the puma and made a noise which seemed to come from the depths of the earth. Mahimbo shivered as it echoed through the forest. But the people of the strange tribe showed no fear.

What was the monkey-man? A god? A spirit? An evil demon? Mahimbo had heard tales of a black puma since childhood. The Elders said it killed for pleasure, paralysing its victims just by looking at them with its icy blue eyes. But here it was quietly standing among all these people. His fear gradually faded. Night was about to fall, and he began to think he would be safer sleeping here than in the forest with all its perils. He decided to come out of hiding.

The strange tribe gave him a friendly welcome. He had only to explain where he came from and why he was there. Then they gave him food and a strong, bitter, grey drink. The whole meal was delicious. As they showed him where to sleep, he spoke to the chief: 'Thank you for everything. I am a stranger but you have treated me as a friend. Forgive me if I ask something.'

'I think I know what is bothering you,' replied the chief. 'You have seen the monkey-man and the black puma. The puma is our god and the monkey-man his friend. Woe to any who harm them!'

All night Mahimbo had strange dreams, and when he woke up he did not remember where he was. Then he sat up in shock. A black shadow was moving at the end of the path.

Then a huge hairy hand grasped Mahimbo's shoulder. He turned, and saw the monkey-man sitting behind him. He seemed to have spent the night by his side. Mahimbo looked carefully at the strange creature, whose gentle eyes seemed to want to say: 'I am your friend. Don't be afraid.' He seemed so sad that Mahimbo was sorry for him.

Then the chief came and said: 'You can talk to him. He understands everything but cannot speak. One day he arrived here, like you did last night, and has stayed with us ever since. He

A huge hairy hand grasped Mahimbo's shoulder. The monkey-man was sitting behind him!

has learnt our ways quickly. When we go hunting in the forest he makes up the fire and rocks the babies. Even the sacred puma has become his friend.'

Mahimbo stayed for breakfast. Before he left he took off his necklace of feathers and seeds and gave it to the chief. He picked up his blowpipe, bow and arrows ready to go home and waved goodbye to his puzzling new friends. As he left he passed the black puma. It gave him an icy look.

Mahimbo was still puzzled days later. If someone else had told him this story he would not have believed it. But he knew he hadn't been dreaming. Everything had really happened.

Now he crossed the clearing and saw the

yellow river which flowed past the mysterious village. A steep slope went down to the dark forest where he had got lost when hunting. He must cross it before sunset, or risk getting lost again.

He walked fast, trying not to slip on the awkward slope. If he were injured, nobody would be able to find him here. Suddenly he heard a noise behind him. He was being followed. He turned and saw the monkey-man.

Mahimbo gulped with fear, but the strange creature was smiling. They walked together down the slope and across the forest. When they reached the river, Mahimbo decided to stop for the night. The monkey-man and he shared some fruit they had collected on the way, then stretched out to go to sleep.

Suddenly two blue eyes pierced the night. The puma had come! Mahimbo was scared, but the puma did not notice him. It turned towards the monkey-man and tapped his shoulder as if to wake him up.

The monkey-man guessed that the puma wanted to take him back to the Sierra, but pretended not to understand. He wanted to go home with his new friend. The angry puma savaged the monkey-man, who howled with pain and fought back. Mahimbo sat still at first, but seeing his friend suffering, he took his bow and shot an arrow straight through the puma's heart.

The monkey-man did not seem glad to be saved; he started to cry. Slowly his sobs became growls – and he became a wild beast again. Something seemed to tell him what to do. He beat his chest with his fists, and began to hit Mahimbo. When the man stopped moving, he threw him into the river and let the piranha fish finish him off.

He had avenged the sacred puma, so that the Sierra tribe would not fall under a curse – but at what cost! As he turned back up the mountain, the monkey-man wondered why the thought of Mahimbo made him sad.

The angry puma savaged the monkey-man, who howled with pain and fought back.

▷ THE AMAZON, THE FOREST AND THE PEOPLE ◁

The Amazon is the second longest river in the world, but by far the biggest system of rivers. A huge network of tributaries – lesser rivers and streams – flows into it, so that it drains an area of about 6 million square kilometres – about four-fifths of the area of the entire USA. It runs through six South American countries: Venezuela, Colombia, Ecuador, Peru, Bolivia and, above all, Brazil. About 25 per cent of the fresh water entering the world's seas comes from the Amazon, which is 400 kilometres wide at its mouth.

The river rises in Peru at 4840 metres above sea level, flows down the eastern slopes of the Andes Mountains and over many rapids to a deep gorge, the Pongo de Manseriche. Below the gorge the river is navigable, and flows through forest.

The Amazon basin has more rain than any area of its size in the world. Scarcely a day passes without rain. During the wettest season the rivers flood the land for up to 60 kilometres on each side. Because of the high temperature and rainfall, plants keep growing all the year round.

The rain forest which covers most of the Amazon basin contains more different species of plants and animals than any other part of the world. It has about 1000 different species per square kilometre. Many are found in the canopy, where the tree-tops merge into a thick layer, shutting out sunlight. There are few ground-living plants (apart from tree trunks) on the dark forest floor, but many climbing plants grow up the trunks, and brightly-coloured 'air plants' live on high branches in the canopy, with their roots taking moisture from the air.

Though vast, the rain forest is disappearing as areas are cleared for grazing, or mining and other industrial processes. Its survival has become an

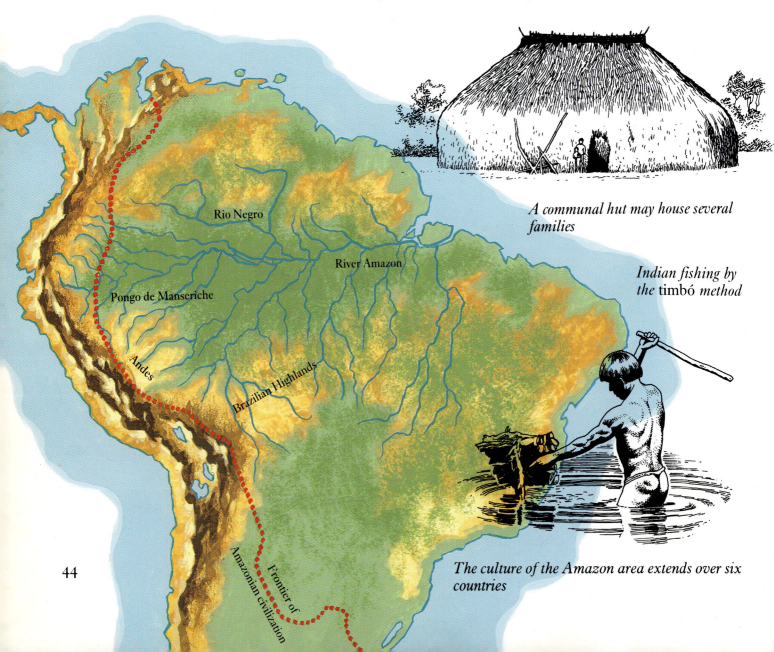

A communal hut may house several families

Indian fishing by the timbó *method*

Rio Negro

River Amazon

Pongo de Manseriche

Andes

Brazilian Highlands

Frontier of Amazonian civilization

The culture of the Amazon area extends over six countries

44

important political issue in South America and the world at large.

Gifts of the forest

Many plants and other products which are now familiar all over the world came originally from the Amazon rain forest: for example, pineapples, avocados and other exotic fruits; chocolate, obtained from the seeds of the cacao tree; brazil-nuts, which grow inside a large, woody fruit; rubber, the sap of a forest tree.

The Indians' knowledge of how to use plant products has given modern medicine valuable drugs; one of the first was quinine, a bark-extract, the first known cure for the killer tropical disease malaria. A root-extract called curare, a deadly poison when used by hunters on arrows, is, when processed, a source of muscle-relaxing drugs used in surgery and to relieve multiple sclerosis and other paralysing diseases.

The forest has an even greater importance to the rest of the world. Animals and humans breathe in oxygen from the air, and breathe out another gas called carbon dioxide. Any sort of burning (in industrial processes and car engines, as well as simple fires) also uses oxygen and produces carbon dioxide. Green plants, on the other hand, take in carbon dioxide to make their own food chemically with the aid of sunlight, and 'breathe' out oxygen. The Amazon forest is the biggest area of green plants on Earth. It quite literally helps provide the air we breathe.

Two Brazilian Indians, Paulino Paiakan and Kube-I, involved in a political campaign against further destruction of the rain forest, recently explained their campaign: '. . . without the forest, we won't be able to breathe, and our hearts will stop and we will die.' This applies to everyone else in the world too.

The people of the forest

Two-thirds of the 120,000 Brazilian Indians alive today are in the Amazon region. Amazonian Indians are generally of medium height; their noses are slightly flattened, and they have high cheekbones, heavy eyebrows, and straight, wiry hair. The men often have long hair, but never wear beards.

The traditional Indian way of life still goes on, though many Indians now work for modern businesses. Where the old ways continue, work is rigidly divided between men and women: for example, in certain tribes, one sex will always plant the crops, the other gather wild fruits from the forest. Both sexes wear few clothes or none, and paint their bodies with plant dyes: red (*roucouo*), blue-black (*genipao*) and sometimes white clay. The red dye is practical as well as decorative; it is a protection against insect bites and is sometimes believed to drive away evil spirits. The people like to adorn themselves with headdresses and jewellery made of feathers, seeds, shells and animals' teeth. They are a cheerful people, who have many ways to amuse themselves. They live in harmony with

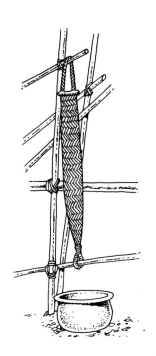

Long basket used to prepare cassava, by squeezing out the poisonous juice

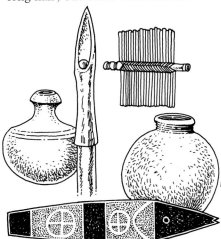

Indians crafts: top right, comb, left and right, pottery, centre, spearpoint, bottom, bullroarer, swung on cord to make a noise

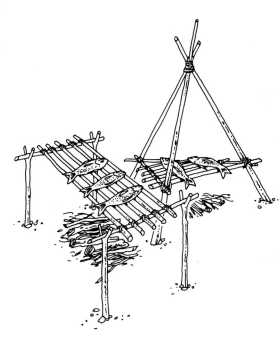

Cooking fish on grills made of sticks. Fish is a major source of protein

the forest, using what it provides without destroying, and have a deep knowledge of forest plants and animals.

The Indians have great respect for their children, whom they rarely mistreat. At the age of ten or so, a child will undergo an initiation ceremony, which makes him or her a man or a woman. Some initiation ceremonies involve difficult feats of endurance.

an important food plant. The Indians squeeze out the poisonous juice in a long basket, leaving the edible starch behind.

Fishing, hunting and gathering fruits and berries are also important to the Indians' economy. Hunters use poisoned arrows and darts, which they shoot with bows or through blowpipes. Bird-hunters use arrows without points, which only stun the birds. The hunter takes some feathers – which are for some tribes the equivalent of money – and lets the bird go.

Fishing is carried out with arrows, harpoons and traps; but the timbó method is the most widespread. A bundle of stems from a poisonous plant (the timbó) is immersed overnight in the river. In the morning, the fisherman comes and beats the bundle with a stick, to make the sap run out into the water. The sap sends the fish to sleep; all the fisherman has to do then is wait a while and take as many as he wants. Fish are often grilled on a sort of barbecue made of sticks.

The River Amazon and its tributaries which provide the fish are also the Indians' major highways. They use canoes and rafts, and boats of balsa wood which are light enough to carry from one river to another.

Many tribes live in communal houses, for several families, with separate entrances for men and women. Sometimes such a house is a village in itself; the Tupinama tribe have houses for up to 200 families. Inside the houses, the furniture and other equipment are very simple: mats and hammocks, baskets and vases.

History and prehistory
The Indians are descended from people who arrived from Asia during the Ice Ages, when the Bering Strait (the narrow sea between Alaska and the eastern tip of the modern USSR) was frozen over. They easily spread all over the Americas, since there were no other people in the continents. These early migrants arrived between 40,000 and 20,000 years ago; the Amazon region was one of the last to be inhabited. The oldest human remains found there are

about 16,000 years old.

Europeans quickly entered South America after Christopher Columbus's voyage there in 1492. The Portuguese explorer Pedro Alvares Cabral is credited with the 'discovery' of Brazil in 1500, and during the next century, the Portuguese colonized the country. Catholic missionaries tried to convert the Indians to Christianity, but found it a hard task in the forests.

From the 1600s, European settlers brought slaves from Africa to work in South American plantations. Black people descended from these slaves are about 25 per cent of Brazil's population today.

Exploration and conquest
The first white man to explore the Amazon basin was Francisco de Orellana. He named the great river after a war-like tribe of women in Greek legends, to commemorate a battle with long-haired (male) Indians.

Stories of cannibal tribes who went about completely naked soon spread throughout Europe – as did the idea of South America as a land of great riches. Gold lured many colonists there. So did the prospect of finding rich spices and other exotic products, previously only available from the Far East. Brazil was in fact named after an Oriental dye-stuff obtained from a tree; a similar substance was found in the Amazon.

In the 1600s, unscrupulous adventurers went right into the depths of the forest in search of valuable woods, of gold and of emeralds. They killed, robbed and enslaved dozens of tribes. More recently, the building of the Transamazonian Highway and new mines have caused the disappearance of whole tribes. And the great rain forest itself is threatened as large areas are cleared for beef grazing.

Culture and religion
Little is known of life in the Amazon region before modern times. Archaeologists have found few ancient remains, because wooden buildings rapidly decay in the hot, damp forest climate. Accounts by early European explorers or colonists also give some

Forest life is based on 'shifting cultivation'. In this type of farming all the trees and undergrowth of a small patch of forest are cut down, left to dry and then burnt. This produces a rich but temporary topsoil, which grows crops for one or two seasons; but eventually the people must move on to another spot, while the cleared forest regenerates.

Cassava, a starchy root which is poisonous without special treatment, is information about Indian life in the past – but compared to the length of the Indians' history, the 500 years since Columbus's voyage are a very short space of time.

The Indians of all tribes share basic beliefs and customs. Tribes separated by huge distances often have their own, slightly different versions of the same myth. Each tribe has a shaman, or

The caracara, a bird of prey, has its own spirit-god too

canoe, or teaching them farming, hunting or fishing.

For the Indians, the world is inhabited by spirits – of rivers, plants or of dead people. Some are kind and some are evil. Each animal is protected by a spirit called its Mother or its Father. The Father of the alligators or the monkeys, say, does not mind if his children are killed for food or in self-

The jaguar-spirit, a terrible enemy if mistreated

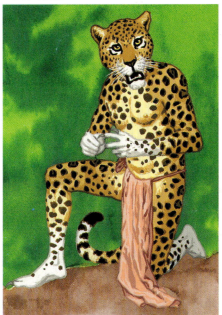

defence, but takes a terrible vengeance if someone kills one to show off his skill as a hunter. This idea has helped to protect animals which are now threatened by modern hunting methods.

There are also spirits of nature, such as the thunder-spirit, master of storms and rain. He is greatly feared, and missionaries tried to identify the Christian God with him.

The hero-spirit is generally accompanied by his friend – a sort of mirror image, who is stupid and blundering where the hero is intelligent. The two together are called the Twins. Their adventures run through most of the Amazonian myths.

Many myths tell how the first people appeared on earth; often they are said to have been created by a god from various materials, or to have come from the sky or from a world under the ground.

The creation of plants is almost as important as that of humans. Some legends have the hero-spirit teaching the Indians to grow crops; others have a hero who changes himself into an edible plant. In some stories all the plants people grow came from a single tree, which sometimes also contains rivers and fish.

Fire and its origin are the subject of many myths. It is never described as something created, always as belonging to an animal or spirit, from whom humans steal it.

Death is portrayed as something that did not always exist, but came into the world as the result of a mistake by the stupid one of the Twins.

Stars and constellations are often featured in myths. Many tribes tell how a star fell in love with a human. Some tribes worship the sun, and there are many stories about the sun and his friend the moon.

There are many stories in which the world is destroyed, by a flood or a great fire, and a man and woman escape to repopulate the world.

All these myths show the Indians' attitude to the world they know: the great green forest, crossed by huge rivers, which is the source of human life, and must be treated with respect.

The Twins – the clever creator-spirit and his blundering brother

witch-doctor, who is an intermediary between people, gods and the spirits of the dead, besides being a healer, adviser, prophet and sorcerer. He keeps the tribe's memory – its traditions. This very important position is usually passed down from father to son.

Most of the Indians believe in a supreme being, who might be a hero or a mythical ancestor. He is credited with bringing a tribe fire, or fruits, or the

INDEX